Hocus Pocus Learn to Focus

Written By Randy Cazell
Illustrated By "Lp"

Acknowledgements

I would like to thank many people who have contributed directly or indirectly to the writing of this book.

First, I would like to thank my granddaughter, "LP", who inspired and created all the characters in this book. She helped the book come to life by her illustrations and creative ideas for each character.

I would also like to thank Gabe, my husband, who has always been a great support and advocate for anything I wanted to try creatively.

I would like to acknowledge the 2007-2008 fourth and fifth grade students at Rich Acres Elementary School for giving me their ideas on how they have been able to conquer their focus problems.

This book could not have been written without the influence of my mother and father, who helped me, as a child, learn to focus and to cope with my own concentration problems.

Last, and certainly not least, I want to thank our Lord, who has led me to this writing.

Randy Cazell

About the Author and Illustrator

The author, Randy Cazell, is an elementary guidance counselor for K-5 students in Henry County, Virginia. She has a special interest in teaching children life skills, and especially HOW to do something. She feels that too many times adults take for granted that children understand concepts like ignoring someone, being confident, studying or focusing. Randy has found that teaching children HOW to do something will enable them to do it with success.

The illustrator, "LP", is a first grade student. She is Randy's granddaughter. The characters and illustrations in this book are created and drawn by "LP".

Both Randy and "LP" hope that this book will help children learn ways to successfully focus in school.

Dedication

This book is dedicated to my family who has always believed in me.

I am also dedicating this book to those children who have not yet mastered the art of focusing and hope that the ideas presented here will help them conquer the frustration of their difficulty with concentrating.

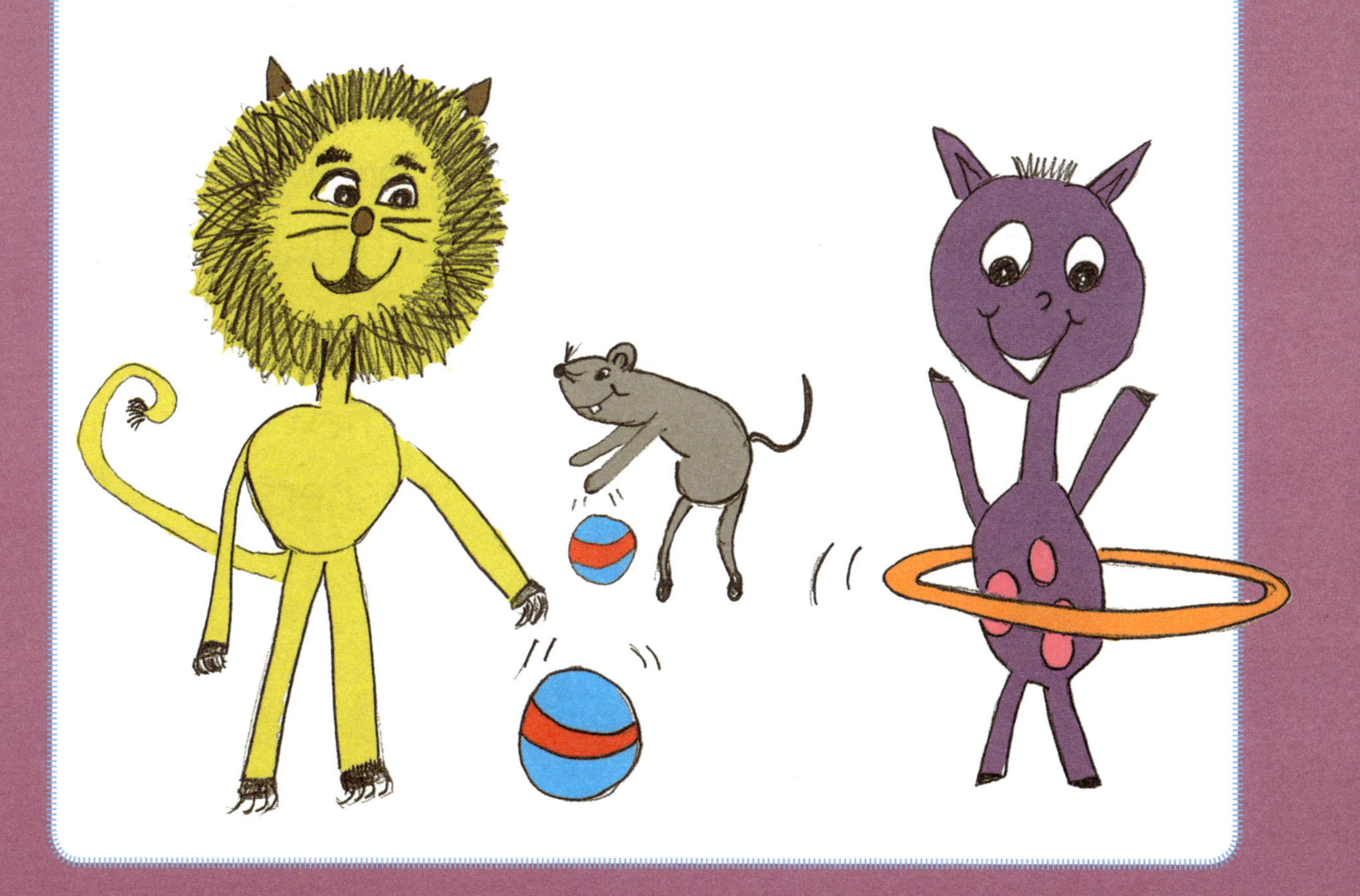

In the small town of Jingle-Jungle there was a school for the animals of the jungle.

Mr. Elmer, the elephant, was the principal of the elementary school. Mr. Elmer loved his school and the children who went there.

Miss Ella was his secretary. She worked with him in the school office. They both helped the teachers at their school.

Mr. Elmer was very smart. He knew how to help the children and teachers.

Jingle Jungle School

Miss Lily Lioness loved to teach.

She had a class of very special children.

They came from all over Jingle-Jungle to be in her class. She had always had a class of students who loved to learn. But this year seemed to be different.

Miss Lily wanted her students to learn, but she noticed they were not paying attention!

"I wonder what is keeping my students from paying attention?" she asked.

Miss Lily noticed that many of the students were not focusing.

A B
C's

Happy Hyena loved to laugh and play!

She was talking and laughing with the students who sat near her in the classroom.

She paid so much attention to the other students that she forgot to listen to Miss Lily or to do her work.

Happy got distracted when she listened to the other students, when she looked at what they were doing and when she thought about what she could do to make them laugh.

She never finished her work.
Happy did not know how to focus.

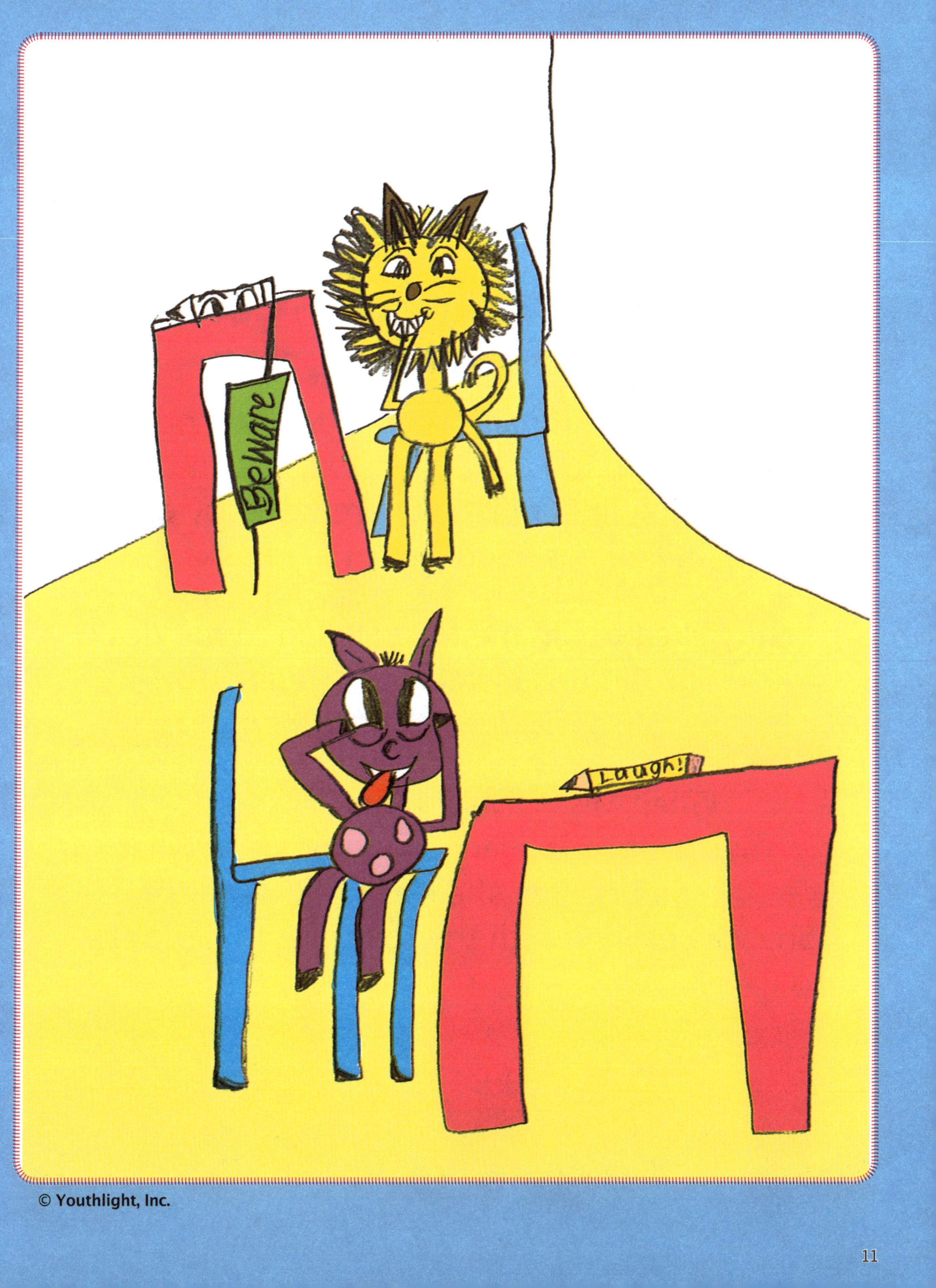
Beware
Laugh!

Miss Lily looked around the class and noticed that Penny Panda was not paying attention either. She was playing with something in her desk. There were toy coins in Penny's hand and in her desk.

Penny liked to flip the toy coins in to her desk. She did this instead of listening to Miss Lily during the lesson.

When Miss Lily told the class to do their seat work, Penny did not know what to do because she was not listening! She was playing with the toy coins in her desk.

There was a noise coming from

the back of the classroom.

"Z-z-z-z-z!! Snort, snort!!"

Miss Lily looked at the back of the classroom and saw Mack the Mouse

sound asleep! He was snoring!!

He was not doing his work.

Instead, he looked like he was having a great dream. Maybe he was dreaming about eating cheese. He was smiling while he was sleeping.

Miss Lily told Leonard the Lion to go and wake Mack up.

"I don't want to wake him up.

It is his job to wake up," said Leonard.

Z-Z-Z-Z-Z-Z-Z

It was a beautiful sunny day.

Miss Lily looked toward the window in the classroom and noticed that Zach the Zebra was climbing onto his desk and was looking out the window. He was not listening to

Miss Lily's lesson either.

"Zach! What are you doing?" she asked.

"Huh? Oh! Ah, I am looking for something!" Zach answered with a startled voice.

"Zach, how can you get your work finished if you do not pay attention?" asked Miss Lily.

Zach was a little embarrassed.

He knew Miss Lily was right.

In the back of the classroom

Tink the Turtle was out of her seat and stood staring at the plant on the back table.

She seemed like she was in another world.

Tink walked s-l-o-w-l-y to get a closer look at the pretty plant. She just stared at the lovely pink color.

Miss Lily stopped what she was doing.

"Tink! Why are you out of your seat?

You are supposed to be working!"

Miss Lily exclaimed.

Tink s-l-o-w-l-y turned around.
When she saw Miss Lily she remembered she was supposed to be working on her seat work.

So Tink s-l-o-w-l-y went back to her desk and got her work out.

5+5=□

As soon as Miss Lily watched Tink

get to work, she noticed another student named Olivia Owl.

Olivia seemed to be having trouble. Her eyes were squinting. She kept rubbing her eyes.

"Olivia, what is the matter?" asked Miss Lily in a soft voice.

Olivia replied, "Miss Lily, my eyes hurt and I can't see the words on my paper very well. They are all blurry. Is there something wrong with the paper?"

Miss Lily knew just what was wrong.

So, Miss Lily wrote today's assignment in VERY BIG letters and gave it back to Olivia.

"Thanks, Miss Lily! Now I can see it! Now I think I can do my work," Olivia told Miss Lily.

Olivia's Day

Suddenly Miss Lily heard a lot of noise coming from the back of the classroom. It was Leonard the Lion growling. Miss Lily watched for a moment and saw Leonard roaring at another smaller student. He was trying to scare the other student. Leonard was very angry.

"Miss Lily, Leonard is being mean again!" several of the students said at the same time. "Leonard Lion, what are you doing? You need to stop that at once! Come up to my desk right now!" Miss Lily said in a very stern voice.

Leonard went up to Miss Lily's desk and as he walked to her desk, he popped each kid he passed on the back of their head!

"Leonard, we do not bully other children in this classroom. You need to concentrate on your work not on how to be mean to others," Miss Lily said in a firm but caring way.

"But everyone is always mean to me at home, so why can't I be mean to everyone here?" Leonard cried with a confused look on his face.

ROAR!!!!!
Beware

The school bell rang

and the students left for the day. Miss Lily was beside herself. She did not know what to do! She had never had such a class as this.

"What am I going to do? If my students cannot focus, they will never learn what they need to know for those important tests at the end of the year. What should I do? I know! I will go and talk to Mr. Elmer about this problem," Miss Lily thought.

Miss Lily went to Mr. Elmer's office.

She was very frustrated.

"None of my students know how to focus! What should I do?" she cried.

Mr. Elmer did not seem concerned.

"I know just what you can do," he told her.

Mr. Elmer picked up his telephone and dialed the number for the Jingle-Jungle Town Magical Garden.

"Brainey Butterfly, please," he said.

"Hello, this is Brainey speaking."

"Brainey, this is Mr. Elmer from the Jingle-Jungle Elementary School. One of my teachers needs your help. Miss Lily's class this year has a terrible problem that I know you can help solve. Her students do not know how to focus!"

"No problem-o, daddy-o Elmer!
You know I have the answer!"
Brainey replied with excitement.

At that, she hung up the telephone, picked up a basket and flew out to the magical garden. She flew over all kinds of beautiful plants and flowers and finally came upon a bright pink and blue flower. There was purple pollen dust in the middle of it and on top of the petals. It was the garden's famous "FOCUS FLOWER!"

Brainey began collecting the Focus Flower Pollen Dust and putting it in her basket.

Each particle of Focus Flower Pollen Dust held special magic that could be sprinkled onto anyone who was having trouble focusing. When the Focus Pollen Dust was sprinkled on them, the jungle animals would instantly understand what they needed to do to focus!

The next morning, taking her basket full of Focus Flower Pollen Dust, Brainey flew directly to Jingle-Jungle Elementary School and right into the window of Miss Lily's classroom.

There Brainey found

Miss Lily's students playing, sleeping, staring, laughing, and growling when they were supposed to be listening. She quietly flew around the classroom spreading Focus Pollen Dust all over the students. As she sprinkled the Focus Pollen Dust on each student she said his or her name and sang, "Hocus pocus, learn to focus!"

Brainey flew by Miss Lily and winked at her. She knew this would do the trick.

The students would now know HOW to focus!

It was amazing! Wonders started to happen! The students quickly figured out what each of them needed to do to solve their own focus problem.

Happy Hyena pretended

she was in a sound proof glass bubble.

She could see Miss Lily but Happy pretended all the other students were invisible. She also pretended her ears only worked when she was listening to Miss Lily. The Focus Pollen Dust filled Happy's ears so she pretended she could not hear the kids. It was like they left the classroom!

Happy put a "privacy folder" on her desk so she could only see her own paper and could not look all around the room or be distracted by the other students.

Then, an interesting thing began to happen. Happy began talking to herself.

She reminded herself to think about her work and to look at her paper until she finished all her work. Then, all of a sudden, she was finished! Happy was really happy and very proud of herself.

I'll Look at my Paper.

When the Focus Pollen Dust landed

on Penny Panda, she had a bright idea. Instead of playing with the toys in her desk, Penny gave her toys to Miss Lily to hold until recess. She also asked Miss Lily to turn her desk around so that she could not even look inside of her desk.

Miss Lily was very pleased when Penny handed her the toys. She knew that Penny would be able to get her work finished now that she didn't have toys to take her mind away from her work.

Mack the Mouse had always fallen

asleep in class. When Brainey dropped the Focus Pollen Dust on Mack, he realized that he was so tired because at home he stayed up late watching TV and playing video games.

In fact, he hardly got any sleep at all at home. That is why he slept in class.

The Focus Pollen Dust landed on Mack's eyes and brain. That night at home he became so tired that he went to bed at 8:00! He even dreamed about school and doing his best in school.

The next morning Mack woke up very rested. He came to school and when it was time to listen to Miss Lily and do his work, he had no trouble at all!

SCHOOL
5 + 5 = □
1 + 1 = □
10 and 2 !!
10 11 12 1 2 3 4 5 6 7 8 9

When the Focus Pollen Dust landed

on Zach the Zebra, like magic he forgot about what was outside the window and he began to think about the work he had to do.
But, he did have to remind himself over and over to look at his paper. He also had to tell himself to look at and listen to Miss Lily and to think about what he was doing.

But, the best thing Zach did to help himself get his work finished was to keep reminding himself every time his eyes drifted toward the window to look out that,
"IF I DON'T GET MY WORK FINISHED,
I WON'T GET TO GO OUTSIDE AND PLAY!"

Zach loved to play outside at school.

If I don't get my work finished I won't get to PLAY!!!

Tink was always in slow motion.

Even the Focus Pollen Dust dropped slowly onto Tink's head. Once it finally landed on her head and onto her brain, Tink was able to focus. But, she had to have a serious talk with herself:

"Tink, think! Think, Tink!

Focus. Keep your eyes on your work. Concentrate!

You can finish and for recess you won't be late!!"

Tink began to imagine being able to finish her work and getting good grades, too.

And, the more she imagined it, the more she was able to finish her work. The more she thought about finishing her work, the harder she worked on it. Then she did it! She got her work finished on time, got good grades AND got to go out to play!

Miss Lily knew why Olivia

could not do her work. Olivia figured it out when the Focus Pollen Dust gently landed on her head and eyes.

"I can't see my work because I can't see the writing on my paper!! When I can't see the letters, my eyes get very tired and it is hard to focus. I am forgetful and I always leave my glasses at home."

Olivia began putting a reminder note in her planner and on the kitchen table that said:
"TO OLIVIA, TAKE YOUR GLASSES TO SCHOOL!
CAN YOU SEE YOUR WAY TO DOING THAT?
LOVE,
ME (OLIVIA)"

It was amazing! Olivia could see her work with her glasses on! (And the kids all thought she was especially cute and smart-looking with them on!) Now she could focus!

I can see because I remembered to bring my Glasses!!

Brainey flew over Leonard the Lion

several times dropping Focus Pollen Dust on him each time. He was a tough case.

Each time Brainey dropped dust on Leonard he seemed to get less and less angry. Finally he looked up at Brainey and said, "I need to talk to someone so I will stop being so mean to others."

Brainey answered, "I know just the place you need to go to do that. You need to go to see Mrs. Gazelle, the school counselor.

She can help you with a speedy answer."

Leonard went to Mrs. Gazelle and talked about his problems. He found out that he didn't have to be mean to others.

When he started treating others nicer, just like a boomerang, the nice treatment came back to him. Then he was able to focus on his work!!

I need to talk to Someone so I Will Stop being mean to others!!!
school
counselor

Brainey had done it!!

She helped all of Miss Lily's students learn the secret to focusing. Each student had to do something different to solve their own focus problem.

But, there was one thing they all could do: NOW THEY COULD ALL FOCUS, FINISH THEIR WORK, FEEL GOOD ABOUT THEMSELVES, AND GET TO PLAY AT RECESS!!

Follow-up Activities

The following pages contain follow-up activities for this story. They are designed to use with kindergarten through fifth grade students. The first page is intended to be used with younger students.

Each page gets progressively more difficult. The activities can be used with individuals, small groups or in the classroom.

The pages can be copied for educational use only.

Questions About the Story

1. What did each student in Miss Lily's class do that kept them from doing their work?

   Happy Hyena
   Penny Panda
   Mack the Mouse
   Zach the Zebra
   Tink the Turtle
   Olivia Owl
   Leonard the Lion

2. What did Mr. Elmer do to help solve Miss Lily's problem?

3. How did Brainey Butterfly help Miss Lily's class?

4. Describe how each student solved their focus problem?

   Happy Hyena
   Penny Panda
   Mack the Mouse
   Zach the Zebra
   Tink the Turtle
   Olivia Owl
   Leonard the Lion

5. Can you think of something else each animal could do?

6. Why did each animal have to try something different to solve their focus problem?

7. Which of the animals in Miss Lily's class are you most like?

8. What can you try to help you focus better in school?

My Plan to Focus

Name ______________________________ Date ______________

Distractions Word Bank

There is noise in the room	Others are talking	There is noise in the hallway
I play with things in my desk	I am with my friends	The work is too hard
I don't understand the work	I daydream	I worry about home
People are picking on me	Others are walking around	I worry about something

My Problem	**My Plan**
It is hard for me to focus when:	When this happens, I need to:
It is also hard for me to focus when:	When this happens, I need to:

After you fill this out, tell it to a partner.
Then share your answers with the whole class.

Get Rid of Those Distractions!!

Name ______________________________ Date ______________

There are many distractions in a classroom. Not all students are distracted by the same things. In order to successfully focus, each type of distraction may need a different solution.

Directions:

1. On your own paper, check those things that distract you and keep you from being able to focus on your work.
2. Add any other distractions you have to the list.
3. Then, with a partner, discuss the distractions below.
4. Discuss with your partner at least two solutions to each focus problem. Get ideas from your partner.

Distraction	Solutions
❑ **Others talking.**	**1.** **2.**
❑ **My own daydreaming.**	**1.** **2.**
❑ **The work is too hard.**	**1.** **2.**
❑ **Thinking about my problems.**	**1.** **2.**
❑ **Thinking about doing something outside or later.**	**1.** **2.**
❑ **Feeling like falling asleep.**	**1.** **2.**
	1. **2.**
	1. **2.**

How I Learned To Focus

PROMPT:

Describe the types of problems you have had with focusing in school. Then describe how you overcame your focus problems. Include how this has affected your school work and success in school.